LECTED POEMS

Selected Poems

CHRISTOPHER LOGUE

*Chosen and arranged by
Christopher Reid*

FABER & FABER

First published in 1996 by
Faber & Faber Ltd
Bloomsbury House, 74–77 Great Russell Street
London WC1B 3DA
This paperback edition published in 2018

Printed and bound by Martins the Printers, Berwick-upon-Tweed

A CIP record for this book is available from the British Library

ISBN 978–0–571–34769–8

10 9 8 7 6 5 4 3 2 1

Contents

Air

Moon and mandrake
Are the fellows
Of this heath

Cairn and gallows
Are the signposts
To this park

Mute and magpie
Are the servers
At this feast

Owl and craken
Are the choir
In this dark.

And Tom Beddoes
Fills the bagpipe
With cracked breath

And leads his bride
And bridegroom
To their death.

Professor Tucholsky's Facts

Once upon a little planet,
a neat, provincial planet, set
deep in the galactic sticks,
there lived an interesting thing
called *Man*.

Man had two legs, and two *Convictions*:
one was called *Luck*,
which he described as *Good* when things went *Right*.
The other one he used when things went *Wrong*.
This was called *Religion*.

Man was vertebrate, bipedic, often bald,
and had a *Soul* that never died.
Also – to check his overconfidence –
he had his *Leaders*, and his *Fellow Countrymen*.

Man ate a lot:
plants, fish, animals, birds, snails . . .
in fact, he ate whatever he could kill.
Occasionally he ate his *Fellow Man* –
but this was rare.

Each man had a liver, a heart, a brain,
and a *Flag*.
These were his vital organs.
On these his life depended.

I have no doubt that there were men alive
with only half a liver;
some had no heart;
and many had no brain.
But a man without a flag?
Impossible!

Man was the most *Useful* of earthly creatures.
Cheerfully he raised the value of shares,
cheerfully he died a soldier's death,
or committed spectacular crimes –
thereby selling innumerable newspapers
all of which have now vanished.

Many admired *Human Character* –
but it was split.
One half was known as *Male*
and did not want to think:
the other half was known as *Female*,
in whom thinking was discouraged.

Yet both had this in common:
they were full of fear.
They were afraid of death, of debt,
of loneliness, of failure, and of war.
But most of all they feared their *Fellow Man*.

Of course, some men were different:
Thinkers, or *Revolutionaries*, or *Saints*.
However, these were few; and they
were quickly crucified, or shot, or poisoned.

Next week we study Dogs.

[3]

The Ass's Song

In a nearby town
there lived an Ass

who in this life
(as all good asses do)

helped his master,
loved his master,

served his master,
faithfully and true.

Now the good Ass worked
the whole day through

from dawn to dusk
(and on his Sundays, too)

so the master knew
as he rode to mass

God let him sit
on the perfect Ass.

When the good Ass died
and fled above

for his reward
(that all good asses have)

his master made
of his loyal hide

a whip with which
his successor was lashed.

A Chorus from *Antigone*

There are many wonders on earth
and the greatest of these is man.
We have divided the world into nations
and we use the land to know
and to nourish ourselves.
Likewise we cross the sea, and the changing air,
as easily as any room—
 even in storms, even at night, for then
we make the white stars guide us through:
indeed, for man, the dark is brilliant, too!
Always the first among living things,
beast, bird, or bug, the changing air, or mineral,
we kill, or catch them out,
we mine them with our cunning hands, until
all that is known is made to obey.
So, in the evening, we sit
by the fire we have tamed,
on the ground we make fertile,
outside, our creature, the horse
that ran wild before we came . . .
Oh, clever us! —
For we have grown inside ourselves,
mind that moves further and faster than light
or the changing air,
and we invented speech
to trap the mind as it flew,
and so to hand things down.
But even as we make, whatever we make,
and no matter how much we make,
we long to destroy the things we have made.

Finding no enemy, we become our own enemy.
As we trap the beasts, so we trap other men.
But the others strike back, trap closing on trap.
Having eaten enough, man next must build a wall
around whatever food is left,
and other men must pull down that wall.
So the roof gets split;
and the rain, and the changing air, wash away
whatever is left of man and his cities,
when men have done with them.

Good Taste

Travelling, a man met a tiger, so . . .
he ran, and the tiger ran after him,
thinking: How fast I run . . .
but the road thought: How long I am . . .

Then they came to a cliff, and the man
grabbbed at an ash-root and swung down
over its edge. Above his knuckles, the tiger;
at the foot of the cliff, its mate.

                      Two mice,
one black, one white, began to gnaw the root.
And by the traveller's head grew one
juicy strawberry.   So . . . hugging the root
the man reached out and plucked the fruit:

how sweet it tasted!

The Song of Autobiography

I came among you in a time of hunger,
Born at daybreak in a dockyards suburb,
Gunboats like grey scum lay on the water.

I, Christopher Logue, was baptized the year
Many thousands of Englishmen,
Fists clenched, their bellies empty,

Walked day and night on the capital city.
In mind this three-year old child walked with them.
This triple step's best foot still must. Amen.

One class gained time. One lost that time.
I asked my mother, who are those men
Singing down the gutter to spoons and little drums?

She said, the out of work and lame.
Lame from what? Lame from war.
In the streets many policemen.

Six. By now the sun and the air had struck
Wealth in my body's side, and: Mother I cried,
Where does that cripple's walk come from?

The open market or work, my son.
His bib went into her bottom drawer. Ask no more,
But agree among you, how, as he slept

Tight as a bean, others born poor
Took picks grey as silver through the level rain
And for pence went mowing or worse.

Nine times November had passed through me when
Germany's iron womb let out its holy man
Whose scourge walked upright round your house,

And rain, moist red, fell through Spain,
Drenching the palliasse, the donkey hurt,
Man, woman and child seen running dead

My father said, and changed his priest. Amen.
I, smug thirteen, talked back: Why fret, old man?
Their black dove works. Engines run dead on time.

Could I give back dead breath so easily yet learn
How the sun was born in a red giant's eye
And Earth was thrown from the sun's gold seed

And my hand was cast while a housewife moaned,
Given ten fingers by the world for free,
Plain bone from which to make poetry.

By August, Sunday, noon, black doves had flown.
I woke. We ate in war. A neighbour said,
What will he do, your pretty boy, to get ahead?

Fifteen I am. To be a man? To get ahead
Is ahead of whom? Whose balding crown shall fall
A little dead to keep me housed and fed?

Neighbour, what is a man? I said.
The fellow died beneath an early bomb
Who said, neighbour, take care your son

Does not grow up to be a trouble-maker.
Away, away, bombed out, I learnt to sing,
Hymns, madrigals, the Ringarangaroo,

Beat and be beaten, play our game, amen,
And we'll play ball with you. Outside
Those eighteenth-century walls, a pyramid

Six million Jewish bodies high lay gassed in shit.
What is a man their shilling soldier cried?
His upper lip gone stiff with keeping

Ten toes against the British party line
Stretched out between Threadneedle Street, the judge,
His priest, our Qu—shut up. As wrong as gold

Her shilling slept for two long years among
The Royal stones of our deep colonial jails.
Home, I climbed a tower in Dorsetshire to see

How far my mind's eye pierced night's cold infinity
And saw, instead of self, the lit peninsulas of Asia
Glint across the downs. The red spark scratched my eye.

If men rebel I must rebel with them and step
My hoity mates into the common time or die. The sea got dark.
When I climbed down the lobster pots were dipped

In their May tar by men I understood because they fished
Out of my country, where to spend a penny means
To piss. Amen. Too pert a truth. But what can three

And twenty do save fall in love? He did? Yes. Yes,
Fell down inside myself because she pushed,
And it was shallow so he bust his conk.

Our last morality called love is cauls alone.
Too private, honey. One plus one makes pain
If either one thinks love the axle

And the stem on which our dumb earth spins.
O Eve, Eve, Eve, give back my soiled rib again,
The full grown child cries. Outside his window-pane

A mile of ghosts passed as the child died,
But he dies hard and we – or is it I and I –
Live out alone. Amen. Amen, again, and

If I dare to say it, yes, amen once more.
Forgive. For when I think of you I am a wren
Who pisses in the sea, every little helps, he says –

So the time passed given on earth to me.
Time tocks and that means work. For whom?
Work means great profit to the mind. Who thrives?

Mind is our finger-tips' true shadow in the brain.
Who profits, buys the fifty-guinea priest
To name and wed and put him in the earth again.

And who may count his blessings is not cursed.
Seven lush meadows my grandma snatched,
Then other greed inspired Sires grabbed back

And built the curious engines they shall loose
This noon. Can I aid that? Alas,
Strife queers my pitch, needs graves.

Meantime I eat and fill myself with hope,
As the time runs given to me on earth.

Envoi

Men of the future think of me
Living at a time when one by one
Our kings gave way to businessmen,
Our poets wrote to make men bother less,
Our wisemen, fat with caution, spoke of death,
And most died twice from individuality,
In this time on earth given by men to me.

The Song of the Dead Soldier

For seven years at school I named
   Our kings, their wars (if these were won)
A boy trained simple as we come,
   I read of an island in the sun,
    Where the Queen of Love was born.

At seventeen the postman brought,
   Into the room (my place of birth)
Some correspondence from the Crown,
   Demanding that with guns I earn
    The modern shilling I was worth.

Lucky for me that I could read,
   Lucky for me our captain said:
'You'll see the world for free my son,
   You're posted to an island, John,
    Where the Queen of Love was born.'

So twenty weeks went by and by
   My back was straightened out my eye
Dead true as any button shone,
   And nine white-bellied porpoise led
    Our ship of shillings through the sun.

We landed with our drums and clad
   In war suits worth ten well-taxed pounds
(The costliest I ever had)
   Our foreign shoulders crossed the town,
    The Queen of Love our flag.

And three by three through our curfew,
   Mother we marched like black and tan,
Singing to match our captain's cheers.
   Then I drank my eyes out of my head
   And wet Her shilling with my fears.

When morning came our captain bold
   Said: 'The island shaped like an ass's skin
Must be kept calm, must be patrolled,
   For outposts are the heart and soul
   Of empire, love, and lawful rule.'

I did not know to serve meant kill.
   I did not see the captain fall.
As my life went out through a bullet hole:
   'Mother,' I said, 'my life is gone –
   Did they spend your English shilling well?'

And then I saw a hag whose eyes
   Were big as medals, grey as lead,
I called my rifle but it was dead,
   Our captain roared but my ears were dud,
   The hag kissed warm, we met in blood,
   English shilling, Queen of Love.

'Loyal to the king'

Loyal to the king
and to preserve
their nationality,
a tribe of nits
inhabiting
the northern cliff of a turd,
from time to time
made war upon
a neighbouring tribe
over matters of territory.

Often among
the conflicting hosts
tens of thousands
of lives were lost.
Sometimes the vanquished were pursued
relentlessly
for up to fifteen days.

A Singing Prayer

By mutual fear
we have come in peace
to the end of the year.

Berries gleam
behind green thorns;
and between our smelly frontiers,
fires burn.

Since we began
three full generations of men ago
what has been done about our references
for the time when Christmas comes for us no more?

A dozen wars
count 50 million dead;
not adding on famine, and plague, and heartbreak.
It is enough to make
the unborn tremble in their wombs.

But do not pretend
that the origin of war is mysterious.
Cross-question those who repeat:
'Disaster is natural to man.'

When you see evil done, do not say:
'It is human nature,'
unless when good is done, you say:
'It is human nature.'

[17]

Why imagine
if a thing happens often, it is natural?
Rather
ask after its kind, and where it started.

And do not find
that you cannot be blamed for a thing;
but that you stand against it.

And if you hear:
'Why bother us with this?' Reply:
'Born with strong noses must cry stinking fish.'

Shun the household
where questions like these, embarrass . . .
In the name of gentility
they ask you to button your lip
when faced by evil.

You will, in any case,
not be asked back.
Yet ask your questions, once.
It is little enough; but something; and
be sure they sleep less tight because you asked.

For the man who is small must think:
'Small acts of goodness are no benefit' –
and does not do them:

'Small acts of malice do no harm' –
and does not abstain from them.
Thus he can tell himself:
'The river moves the river on.'
Combing his hair each day, but not his heart.

Observe the acts of those who claim
to be above such things.
Notice the deeds of who insists
injustice bores her.

And
if you pray,
do not rest content with your prayers.

It is hard – I know.
Cold comfort – I know.
And if you came to me you would find
a man needing much forgiveness.

Indeed, I would like to change; to be wise.
And I have been told that wisdom consists
of avoiding strife.
To dig my own square inch till it bears
apples in March, is held to be wise.
'Be still,' such wisdom says, 'and when
your neighbour's beard goes up in flames
moisten your own. Make no attempt
to actualise your dreams; but call them vanity,
and lose your shame in compromise.'
Alas, I can do none of these things.
It cannot be said that I am wise.

Well over half our century is gone.
We were three generations
possessing opportunity and time
who were too much possessed by them.

Our inheritance contained
much that was wrong;
yet it cannot be said
we were born empty-handed.

Easily persuaded to slay each other,
among us those who profited from slaughter
lived in peace.
So we made tolerance a vice.

Infinitely careful of each self,
we stood for liars in public places;
and called it freedom,
because we did not have to hear them.

When you ask after us and find
weakness, falsehood, malice, pride,
and the complex excuses we made about them,
judge us – but with forbearance.

For if we did not seek out
the evil among us too carefully,
nor did we rest in peace.

Take what is best for keeps;
keep what was worst in mind;
for we who measured time by pain
never will return again;
and more than half our time is gone.

I wrote this song
for those who will be born
in the time we call New Year,
to be among you there,
even as you are here.

The song is given away
like a man's top-coat when he dies,
who knew it cost too much
for him not meant to last,
and knowing this would make
the same mistake again.

What peace can the living have
when the dead have none?
Agree among you.
Here we three are one.

For My Father

A year ago tonight my father died.
   Slow on the year, you bells,
   slow on the year . . .
And, Master Sun, as you have met your prime
   and sit
   high in the Lion's house
and have no shadow in your courtyard,
   bequeath
some brief alliteration of your radiance
   to glint this work in words
   that speak of ghosts.

Hector, is Hector dead: and so is he.
His breath, some feathers for an ocean mew;
his hand, his parting wave, some moment where
a rowan's leaf disturbs its morning dew.

'Arrested by mistake – not so released –
   be sure you pray.
No losing throw like hate –
   so keep to love.
Who injures you, will not forgive his blow:
   so you must fight.
The wise read letters backwards.
   You must learn.
Your hands are not on loan –
   so you must work.'
Salute, you lucky mourners, all the dead,
   by your attention this day,
   for you must think.

[22]

Lean priest had not his love
at our last meeting in a London church.
Nor I, nor anyone could lend
a meaning to that requiem
beyond the painful oak.

The host was memory; the wine
examination of the way he grasped
a problem by its rim.
This double sacrament calls in
an Irish Englishman, a dusty road,
his hat tipped halo back, his stick;
Belloc and Chesterton – their verse,
and RLS – his prose.
And never in his life a truthless word;
indeed, which vexed his boy,
a certain scorn of words; a greater joy
in notes well sung, a stone well thrown,
fine horses managed by a careless rein.
And never in his life a truthless word,
an unjust blow, a mawkish saint.
Vengeance, unknown; unknown, complaint:
'It was unjust!' 'So I have heard you say.
Think of the justice done you, child. And pray.'

Ground, cover him.
Sky, tuck the reflection
of his coffin's lid
into that sparrow's wing.

'Write what you like.
Do something to make other people laugh.
And if at nothing else – at you.
Your temper, boy, will get you thrashed
before you're through.
I cannot bless your Mr Shakespear. True,
he can say it all. And yet
imagine him this afternoon:

*The Tragedy of Hitler. Act One, Scene One.
Enter two officers . . .*
Poo poo.'

   Spider,
how can I get his most, most gentle voice,
   across the sacrament of death?
   Ant,
from the spire of that grassblade,
can you see larger absences than his?
   Blackbird
behind the maybloom, what is there new
beside the pearly wake of snails,
for me to write upon this paper stone?
'Ah!' he would say, 'you should have heard me sing,
before I broke my shoulder whistling.'

   Facts fail. The nave grows dim.
   They buried him in rain.
   It cost my mother £50.

   Now we drink sherry
   and recount his worth,
   in this first dusk
   I am alone on earth.

September Song

Be not too hard for life is short
And nothing is given to man.
Be not too hard when he is sold and bought
For he must manage as best he can.
Be not too hard when he gladly dies
Defending things he does not own.
Be not too hard when he tells lies
And if his heart is sometimes like a stone,
Be not too hard, for soon he dies,
Often no wiser than he began.
Be not too hard for life is short
And nothing is given to man.

The Song of the Imperial Carrion

Not long ago
on the northern shore of the Black Sea
lived many birds and fishermen.
Many birds, but no vultures.

Early one morning
soldiers came,
brave men led on by gentlemen.
A week, and most lay dead among
dead birds, dead fishermen.

And before another
week was out,
as if they smelt the English dead
some thousand miles off,
from Africa the vultures came.
Perhaps the wind blew south.

Winter cleaned out
what soldiers there were left.
Only a few
vultures followed the army's ships.
The rest built nests.

So the community of birds
on the northern shore of the Black Sea
increased by one.
And those who go
fishing along that coast today
call that bird the English crow.

As you go to bed
consider the English crow. He flies
like a flag a thousand miles wide
for the soldiers and the fishermen who died
on Her Majesty's Service.

To My Fellow Artists

Today, it came to me. How you, my friends
who write, who draw and carve,
friends who make pictures, act, direct,
finger delicate instruments,
compose, or fake, or criticize – how,
in the oncoming megaton bombardments
all you stand for will be gone
like an arrow into hell.

It is strange, and yet
if I tell you how the sunlight glitters
off intricate visions etched into breastplates
by Trojan smiths, you say: Yes! Yes!
And if I say:
Around my bedposts birds have built their nests
that sing: No! No!
or say: When I flog salt, it rains;
when I sell flour, it blows –
you feel my hopelessness,
you understand my words.

But if I speak straight out, and say:
Infatuates to local immortality,
distinguished each from each by baby pains
you measure against baby pain, you stand
to lose the earth and look alike
as if you spat each other out, you say:
Logue grinds his axe again. He's red –
or cashing in . . .   And you are right:

I have an axe to grind. Compared to you,
I'm red. So what?
I think, am weak, need help, must live,
and will – with your permission – live.
Why should I seek to puzzle you with words
when your beds are near sopping with blood?
And yet I puzzle you with words.

If (as many as you do) you base
all of your hope, all of that hope
necessary to make a work of art
on unborn generations,
start hunting for a place to hide the work
you will create in privation.

Consider, my fellows,
how all the posh goodies inside our museums,
stones, books, things we have stolen,
think of them turned to instant dust
one dusk between six and six-ten.

It is true: they will say you are fools
who know nothing of politics.
Women and artists must keep out of politics.
They will suggest (politely . . . politely . . .)
that the length of your hair pre-empts your sanity.
They will, with their reason,
prove your unreasonableness;
though you are drugged by rationality.

Listen, I beg you. Six days ago
a paper called the *Sunday Times*
revealed, with witless candour,
their foul thoughts:

You are confused about destruction, yes?
they said. And then – recommending the death of the country
in the name of the country: *We shall bomb,*
if bomb we must, bomb like King Billy,
for the British have something to die for.
No mention was made of something to live for.
Saying (in the names of loyalty, faith, integrity):
How vile they are who wish to live here
minus democracy.
Not speaking of those who wish to die here.

The death before dishonour, boys;
the death before gestapo, boys;
the death before a tyrant, boys;
the death before the *Sunday Times.*

But where is the dishonour, gestapo, or tyrant?
And who wants to dishonour or govern a cinder?
My friends,
how difficult it is for those who speak out of anger
to answer those who speak out of complacency.

And yet, imagine a horror
and perpetrate horrors because of it,
is called mad.

Think desolation
and create desolation because of it,
is called mad.

Thus they think of our country.

So do you agree with them,
Spender, and Barker, and Auden?
And you, my newly married master, Eliot –
will you adopt their lie by silence,
and having sold our flesh to war
bequeath our bones to God?
Or are there two sides to *this* question?

But I fear we are easily beaten.
So where shall we hide them, our treasures?
Uncertain the disused chalk pit;
uncertain the bank's steel vault;
and the holds of ships are uncertain.

We must beg for permission
to hang our paintings underground,
to store our books and stones in mines:
But the rents will be high underground,
and I doubt if we can afford them.

Perhaps they will let a few of us hide
in the negative silos, 1000 feet down,
where, beside telephones, uniformed men
await fatal words.
We must not be afraid to ask;
for works concerning the private heart
will not faze those devoted carers.

But let us remember to leave behind
permanent signs. Signs that are easily read.
Signs that say: So deep,

beneath this many feet of stone,
is a poem expressing refinement of taste,
a book about logic, a tape of quartets,
and a picture of the painter's wife.

Then can our six-handed grandsons,
our unborn consolation,
discover that we too, had art.
And those who dare look
over the crater's jagged rim,
may, in the evening, climb down
into the mauve bowl of London,
and dig.
While their guards watch out
for tyrants, and food, and sun.

Think, men of no future,
but with a name to come.

Observe Details

When you visit the Humans
who stick to their fruitless cinder,
be sure to see,
down by the nice little bar where they sell
roast mutton and girls,
the armless Army man who sings
'How Tranquil the Evening'
as he points his leg at the moon.

'When I was serving my country'

When I was serving my country
a staff-sergeant said:

> There's dozens of ways, but if everything fails
> put your head on her shoulder
> your prick in her hand,
> and cry.

He slept on the bunk above me in Wrexham,
and what he said was true.

> Christ,
said the boy who got into Airborne
and died outside Caen,
> when you're coming you wish your pipe was a mile long.

His hair was yellow. He came from Stroud.
And what he said was true.

On the way to Port Said they showed me a photo:
an overhead shot from the side of a troopship
moored in the roads of Singapore harbour.
On the water below us,
a two-eyed bumboat heaped with souvenirs;
and in its bows a woman, naked, arms upspread,
holding the seamed edge of a muslin sheet
that billowed outwards from her hands, and tugged
against the regulation belt strapped around her hips.

I am for sale, too!
they said she cried.
She must be dead by now.
And I am sure that what she cried was true.

'His case is typical'

His case is typical.
On leaving school he showed no tendency to seek
honest employment.
I visited him often.
I formed the opinion that he was not
inherently vicious. However,
during his formative years something had snapped.

He thought everyone was against him.
He took a dislike to his Chaplain.
He failed to draw strength from the Bible.

Though the guards showed him nothing but kindness,
he made no attempt to lighten their task.
He sulked. He was bitter.

And on the last day when the privilege to choose
a reasonable menu is given to those who must die,
he neglected the offer.
He sat saying nothing.

I asked him to listen. I said to him: Lad,
wait till the cyanide egg hits the acid,
then draw a deep breath;
trying to help him in spite of his coldness.

Next day I had a visit from his mother.
You were doing no more than your duty, Governor.
You did your best. You have his mother's thanks.

Your boy was one of my failures, Ma'am.
How could he think the world was against him
with someone like you at his back?

'A middle-aged man is approaching an all-night lavatory'

A middle-aged man is approaching an all-night lavatory.
Passing a twelve-wheel lorry roped with green tarpaulins
he goes downstairs, selects a cubicle, and sits.

Someone rustles in the neighbouring cubicle.

The wood partition and the tiled floor
are separated by a four-inch gap.

The first arrival slides his foot towards the gap.

Mechanical faucets drench the line of porcelain stalls.

The man who passed the lorry on his way
removes his shoe and sock,
the other one goes down upon his knees
seizes the foot and smothers it with passionate caresses.

A minute afterwards he tucks
a banknote in the sock and leaves.
His knees are damp.
Words like GRAVE, CASE and LURID CHARGES
roar in his mind. When he was young
he made a candlestick on his own lathe.

Lullaby

Here is the trapdoor,
here is the rope,
here is the convict,
here is the judge and
here the skilled hangman;
here is a juror,
   and eleven more
   sensible humans
   not courted before.

Here is the judgment,
here is the crime,
   go from the prison
   into the lime.
Here are three Sundays,
here is the Warden,
here is the Chaplain,
   and coming behind him
   the convict's weight
   and how he will die;
   dutiful lights
   in the hangman's eye.

Here is the throat;
here is the knot
   as long as your forearm;
here is the spring from
here to eternity
   dressed in a hood.

And be it a man
or a woman they shit
and they come
as they swing
and the soul goes adrift.

Here is the hangman,
here is his garden,
here he is sleeping,
this is his number.
    And one of the jurors
    has given a daughter
    to comfort his slumber.

The Song of the Outsider

This city and its citizens are green.
Quickly, those who come from far off
and enter this city, turn green.
Many have rushed here, suffering dangers unnumbered,
just to be green. And others, with contacts,
with money, with skills that are wanted,
have brought their children, dogs and servants,
so that all they possess shall be green.
Only one dweller herein,
only one, has not become green.
How much he would give to be green!
If he could be green, why – nothing would matter.
He suffers from this. He may well go *Pop!*
At night, beneath the huge green stars,
he goes about crushing young greenies
to ease his hatred and fears.
It is bad to do this. He knows it is bad.
And thinking of his evil deeds he sheds
deeply felt tears. 'If only I were green,' he says,
'life would be like a children's game.'

I Shall Vote Labour

I shall vote Labour because
  God votes Labour.
I shall vote Labour in order to protect
  the sacred institution of The Family.
I shall vote Labour because
  I am a dog.
I shall vote Labour because
  upper-class hoorays annoy me in expensive restaurants.
I shall vote Labour because
  I am on a diet.
I shall vote Labour because if I don't
  somebody else will:
  AND
I shall vote Labour because if one person does it
  everybody will be wanting to do it.
I shall vote Labour because if I do not vote Labour
  my balls will drop off.
I shall vote Labour because
  there are too few cars on the road.
I shall vote Labour because I am
  a hopeless drug addict.
I shall vote Labour because
  I failed to be a dollar millionaire aged three.
I shall vote Labour because Labour will build
  more maximum security prisons.
I shall vote Labour because I want to shop
  in an all-weather precinct stretching from Yeovil to Glasgow.
I shall vote Labour because
  the Queen's stamp collection is the best in the world.

I shall vote Labour because
    deep in my heart
I am a Conservative.

To a Friend in Search of Rural Seclusion

When all else fails,
  Try Wales.

The Story of the Road

Imagine yourself in a country, poor –
not as ours is – but poor for better than bread.
Some men have not worked for ten years, and some
(the youngest) never.
There are many priests hereabout. Some, good men,
some pleased to bless the Lord Mayor's goat, in a land
shaped like a triangle, set in known water,
host to a host, but owned by less than 1000 men
from its limestone base to the cone at its top,
to the water's edge and beyond.

Well, one day, off the weekly boat
that brings mail, tobacco, and news,
a man called Daniel came to see
where his father had worked on the railway.
A girl was having her third by the pump,
and it died by the pump while Daniel looked,
shook his big head, walked by, and later that day
rented a house in the stinking quarter,
and wrote to his girl:'Either come, or it's off.'

It is March. Early spring. Some buy cheap meat.
When it boils you scent their extravagance.
And all day long this Daniel poses questions:
such as when, for how long, for how much, and for whom
(aside from themselves) they fish. And they said:
'We do not flinch at the shadow of a whip,
or the whip . . . So the child died? So what? We are brave.'
And Daniel (who is cautious) saw their courage

and was glad; but also saw their trembling hands.
A message came that night. It said:'I am on my way.'

Long night. No moon. Still blackness round
the low white houses with wide throats.
Wise people sleep. But some (not always young)
with energy enough to scorn their pain,
sit listening while the fish thieves trawl the coast
and the newly spawned are caught with the two-years-old
and the autumn shoal is lifted in the spring.

Six weeks of questioning and soon
wherever Daniel goes many children go
and not a few police. One unemployed fisherman said:
'Statistic? What's a statistic? 'Well . . . from this town
350 unemployed fishermen got
3000 years of gaol between them but
only 50 years of school between them.'
Even the chief policeman laughed, till Daniel said:
'Tomorrow we strike – yes?' 'Yes.' They wrote that down.

Some people had said: 'He will stay for a week.
He will stay for a month. He will starve –
for poverty's catching.'
But the almonds had turned when he said:
'Tomorrow we strike – yes?' 'Yes.' Tomorrow it was.
Around dawn. When it rains.

Some who had never gone striking before, were shy
and said to themselves: What good can it do?
Some told themselves that Christ, in time, would come
and just as he made bread, make work.
And some were scared or finished with the world.

But when those who were scared, or shy, or sure, were gone,
those who were left went down to sit
all through the night on the beach like one big stone,
without eating, together,
because Daniel said it was best
if everyone dwelt on the matter in hand.
So we sat.

Then, around four, Daniel stood up and said
why we, workless people, were here and on strike.
And how, in two hours' time, we would walk
six miles inland and work, for nothing,
all day long repairing the inland road,
without breakfast, leaving our knives behind
in case there was trouble.

Half six. No cockcrow yet. The morning star
half hidden in the rain. We prayed a bit,
and Daniel repeated our reason for striking:
Not as a symbolical, but a normal action.
Not for money, but to show we can work.
And that not to work is a crime against oneself. Yes,
Tuesday we fast, Wednesday we feast off work,
and we moved off, 300 men like an ant
trundling a stone eight times bigger than itself.

One man, a carter, who came from a street
with 30 people in gaol for murder
and had no good reason to strike except
that his mother insisted, sang:
   O moon, O moon,
   O soldier moon,
   I had rather you at my back tonight

than the King and all his cavalry.
Which was fine – except there was no moon.

A mile from the beach we split,
going different ways to the place we had chosen
so as not to disturb the police.

Seven. Less rain. Now and again the sun looks through,
glints off the mattocks as we pile the stones
bigger than melons along the verge.
Mud to your knees, but the work goes well.
50 yards cleared in under an hour.
Nine. The sound of lorries on the coastal road.
Will they pass or turn? Will they wait in the village,
or come to us up the inland road.
They turn. They come as near as they can. The police.
700 of them. With guns.

Now the rain has stopped and by ten
we have cleared a little more of the road,
when a fine-boned, short, well-perfumed man,
twirling a little pistol on his forefinger,
stepped down to us and said:
'Stop work. I order it. Stop work.
Just stop this work at once. Or else we shoot.'

We did not stop.

'Say nothing,' Daniel said, and his whisper stood.
Then the well-boned man fired once into the sun,
and Daniel said: 'We shall sit down and rest.'
So all sat down. In the mud and wet.
You could see your face in the pools.

11 a.m. And the short man said: 'You see this whistle? Well,
when I have blown it twice you will go home.'
Then blew, and blew. Still no one moves.
And so, led by the fine-boned man they pushed
among our faces with their knees
and stood round Daniel, saying: 'Up. Or else.'
And Daniel lay down flat. So it was else.
'Pick him up,' their leader said, and they, poor chaps,
they tried. But Daniel is six plus,
and, well . . . not thin; not thin at all; and they,
poor chaps, are not paid much;
and most of that goes on the uniform.
It took seven men who got dirty as hell
to carry him, face downwards, to the truck.

And the charge against him and the rest, was:
Trespassing on public property.
And eight of us (with Daniel and the carter) got
ten years apiece and shared a cell
with eight condemned to death for banditry
watching a pair of cats make love on the roof
while the wireless gave a boxing match.
And over the courthouse porch was carved
    OMNIA VINCIT AMOR
'Don't you fret,' the warder said,
'You're not like them.' (The bandits.) 'I bet this –
by the time they're shot, you're out.'

And a number of famous artists came; wise men,
whom Daniel trusted. And the Communists came,
and made a great to-do up the leg of the land,
and got a Deputy in on the strength of it.
And we got out.

Late autumn. Home. New bread. Good wine.
Better of course than the gaol where old men pine
for the end of their breath.
But the inland road is still a rut,
and half of those who struck went north,
and the fish thieves thieve,
and the red leaves shine so bright
they scorch the wings of passing birds.

'Cats are full of death'

Cats are full of death.
Horses
and even very small dogs
scare me.
I fear I am not very English.

Lately, however,
a mouse has come to live in my flat.
At 40, pushing 41,
a man who lives alone
and breaks his teeth while eating jam
is, is he not,
rather ridiculous?
So I am grateful.

I eat at home more often,
compose with greater ease,
and yesterday I bought a book on mice.

All things considered,
my mouse is very fortunate.
Though poor, I have expensive tastes.
My mouse has camembert and b rie in peace,
whereas some mice of my acquaintance run
fantastic risks
for lumps of sweaty cheddar.

I must admit he's not all that intelligent.
The first time I saw him

walking down the middle of the room,
tail in the air –
tra-la!
– I thought he was brave.
Now I realize he had lost his hole.
Later I discovered he had only one eye, and,
needless to say,
posh vets won't have him in their surgeries.
What's more,
Madame won't like him.

But what can you do? –
he has moved in
and she hasn't.

Caption for a Photograph
of Four Organized Criminals

This is the final statement we shall make:
Although we got no less than we were due,
Pity the likes of us, and God may take
Pity, my friends, upon the likes of you.
Observe us in the middle of the air;
Four rashers off a putrid barbecue;
The stink alone is half enough to scare
You out of all the wrongs you long to do.
So lift your honest eyes to Heaven and swear:
Be good to us — and we'll be true to You.

Your kids became our addicts, and our whores;
We broke your strikes; and, when the need arose,
We bought your officers, we bent your laws,
How many witnesses we slew, God knows —
You stupid, vain, selfrighteous, ugly bores!
We, the dynamic impresarios
Who gratified your soft, incarnate flaws.
If you should feel some recompense is due,
Mention us when you make that deal of yours:
Be good to us — and we'll be true to You.

Gas, gunshot, Alcatraz, the electric chair —
Only the best machinery could do
Justice to the sensational despair
You legal felt for us illegal few.
Please do not let such absolutions numb
Your dreaming hearts; it is high time you knew,
From Paradise to Pandemonium

There's but one make of different men, not two,
Crying outside the gates of kingdom come:
Be good to us – and we'll be true to You.

Remember this, good men who passed your time
Securely chained while squealing to be free:
Without society there is no crime,
And without crime there's no society.

'I've worked here all my life'

'I've worked here all my life.
The new machines need fewer hands
so this is my last week.

My job was threading up.
That is to say the sets came down the belt,
as they passed me by
I put a green wire through four yellow beads.

The belt went by for years.
And if I wasn't thinking other things
I used to wonder what its colour was.
The sets were packed so tight you couldn't see.

Last week when it stopped I found out.
It was black.'

'Madam'

Madam
I have sold you
an electric plug
an electric torch
an electric blanket
an electric bell
an electric cooker
an electric kettle
an electric fan
an electric iron
an electric drier
an electric mixer
an electric washer
an electric knife
an electric clock
an electric fire
an electric toothbrush
an electric razor
an electric teapot
an electric eye
and electric light.
Allow me to sell you
an electric chair.

Chinese England

Hilltops seen through rain and cloud.
On his way home the angler feels
the weight of his clothes.

Songs from *The Lily-White Boys*

*The Young Hero Sings
a Song of Self-Understanding*

Tonight, the young but rotten are on view,
Though this, my friends, is your first chance to see
Precisely what it is they think of you.
That's fair – you'll all agree?
Will anyone who feels it isn't true
Please answer: Me!

Blind-worms we come.
Wise rats we go.
What else can you do?
Perhaps there's some way out.
I'd like to know.
Is there a good man in the house?

You tell us that the world is split in two,
And our half stands for opportunity,
So when war starts we'll fight and die for you.
But while our half is free
It seems that it's my neighbour I must knife
Or he'll knife me.

Blind-worms we come.
Wise rats we go.
What else can you do?
Perhaps there's some way out.
I'd like to know.
Is there a good man in the house?

We're mean enough to pick up what we spit,
For watching what you do, my friends, we know
That helping's dead and living's very sick . . .
O . . . very, very sick . . .
However, in our case, let's hope life yields
Some money quick.

Blind-worms we come.
Wise rats we go.
What else can you do?
Perhaps there's some way out.
I'd like to know.
Is there a good man in the house?

The Song of Natural Capital

My mother said:
It doesn't pay to educate a girl.
What good is history in bed?
Women have got their natural capital.
Love comes to all
At one time or another,
Those in satin, those in shoddy.
Love is all very well
Said my mother
But a girl's best friend's her body.

Thirty-eight, twenty-four, thirty-nine,
Golden flesh and touchable line,
Forty-one, twenty-four, forty-two,
Eyes that match emerald blue,

Thirty-five, twenty-four, thirty-three,
Bum like a twisted cherry . . .
   Ah me . . .
   Ah me . . .

Wise men have said
That beauty is its own reward, yet they
Don't work but only sleep in bed.
Women depend on making beauty pay.
Men come to all
At one time or another,
Some men bully, some come crying,
Men are all very well
Said my mother
And they make love sound inviting.
But you climb life's ladder on your back,
So get their promises in writing.

Thirty-eight, twenty-four, thirty-nine,
Golden flesh and touchable line,
Forty-one, twenty-four, forty-two,
Eyes that match emerald blue,
Thirty-five, twenty-four, thirty-three,
Bum like a twisted cherry . . .
   Ah, me . . .
   Ah, me . . .

The Girls' Spare Chorus

Just let a man into your house
And he will want your bread,
Just give him bread inside your house
And he will want your bed,
Just let him lie upon your bed
He'll make himself your mister,
Then when he's rested and well fed
He'll seduce your sister.

Go to the Wall

When I was young I often heard
That virtue was its own reward,
And every day at school they'd teach:
Do what is right – all will be well.
So it can do no harm to tell
The fate of those who practise what they preach.

My father wanted to do right.
They said: Improve your mind!
He worked all day and read all night
And now he's proud of being blind.
   Right gets you nowhere,
   It goes on, that's all, my darling –
   Those who trust in being right
   Go to the wall.

My brother said: I'll prove it true
That might is right is wrong.
The mighty beat him black and blue
And proved that he was born a gong.
  Truth gets you nowhere,
  It goes on, that's all, my darling –
  Those who live to tell the truth
  Go to the wall.

My teacher said: The rich will fall
If men unite their claims.
They chained my teacher to the wall,
And now she loves her chains.
  Men can change nothing,
  They go on, that's all, my darling –
  Those who put their trust in men
  Go to the wall.

And now you tell me love provides
More calories than cream!
O, better a slice of bacon, love,
Than a fat pig in a dream.
  Love gets you nowhere,
  It goes on, that's all, my darlings,
  Those who put their trust in love,
  Go to the wall.

The Chorale

You have seen us come from nothing,
Seen what industry can do,
And in spite of good intentions,
We're successful – just like you.

We were rebels when we started,
Champions of boot and cosh,
Next we worked to earn our money,
Now our money works for us.

Time to go now, time to tell you
Life is short and men are fools,
Fall in love, but don't ask questions,
Pay your taxes, keep the rules.

When the future finds you wearing
Plastic teeth and borrowed hair
And you're begging God for mercy
Don't forget us in your prayer.

Come to the Edge

Come to the edge.
We might fall.
Come to the edge.
It's too high!
COME TO THE EDGE!
And they came,
and he pushed,
and they flew.

Rat, O Rat . . .

never in all my life have I seen
as handsome a rat as you.
Thank you for noticing my potatoes.

O Rat, I am not rich.
I left you a note concerning my potatoes,
but I see that I placed it too high
and you could not read it.

O Rat, my wife and I are cursed
with the possession of a large and hungry dog;
it worries us that he might learn your name –
which is forever on our lips.

O Rat, consider my neighbour:
he has eight children (all of them older
and more intelligent than mine)
and if you lived in his house, Rat,

ten good Christians
(if we include his wife)
would sing your praises nightly,
whereas in my house there are only five.

The Aardvark

Into the moonlit midnight,
Out of his stateless hole,
Set for an insect intake
A common aardvark stole.

Depict this common aardvark:
Globe eyes of fiery rose;
Long of tail, of tongue, of ear;
Yet longer still of nose.

He sniffs the ermine moonshine;
He hears the vermin snore;
Brisk as a whip the aardvark's tongue
Streaks from the aardvark's maw ...

GIGANTIC LICK SNUFFS GLOW-WORM!
MIDGE-CLOUD ENGULFED MID-AIR!
Followed by half a thousand ants
(An aardvark's normal fare),

A myriad of rotifers
Cruising a humid nit,
Another half a thousand ants
(To keep him fat but fit),

An ounce of infant locusts,
A cache of millipedes,
Another half a thousand ants,
And then? – ah, then he needs

Rest on the trek through hunger
To woo his mortal soul.
Meekly the common aardvark
Goes back into his hole.

The Isles of Jessamy

'Twas on the good ship Dollymop,
The crew made no attempt to stop,
Their Captain drinking hynopop,
　　Known as the Merman's Tea.

He climbed the mast and shouted: 'Mark,
Leewards the highbrowed *Cutty Sark*.
Quiet as the fin of a tiger shark
　　She parts the sunlit sea.'

'Do not mislead us with your woe,
Dear Captain,' sighed the Mate, 'we know
The little shirt you mention-o'
　　(The crew wept openly)

'Went down a thousand days ago:
Each wax-stitched inch of calico,
And all aboard her, lie below
　　The Isles of Jessamy.'

Larboard the mast their Captain drew.
Then doffed his bowler as he flew.
Back from the white horizon's blue
　　They caught his: 'Goodbyeee . . . '

Since when his shipmates sail the lanes
That slate the great abyssal plains
Where none may stay until she gains
　　The Isles of Jessamy.

Things

The sun shines on the fields and on the town.
Far in the distance by the mill
A man in blue is gardening.
A cat sleeps on a window-sill.
At a bar, two gentlemen discuss the latest Aston-Martin.

A boy and girl by a railway bridge.
The girl holds up her face. Is kissed.
The train that passes by contains
A general and a scientist
Delighting in each other's brains.

In a quiet place a woman of fifty dressed in black,
With a newspaper across her face,
Dreams that she is young and slim.
The front page of the paper says:
   I MARRIED A SEXUAL MANIAC
And the back page says:
   SKIRTS WILL BE SHORTER IN THE SPRING.

The lovers go their separate ways.
She feels he only wants one thing.
He feels he's misunderstood.
The man who has been gardening
Cleans his spade with a bit of wood.
And the sun goes down on the fields and on the town.

Air for the Witness of a Departure

A high wind blows
over the long white lea
lover
O lover
over the white lea.
Knows
who knows where my love is riding?

Thrush in the maybloom
high winds blow
O
over the long white lea.
Knows
who knows where my love is riding? –
thrush in the maybloom
riding
riding
over the long white lea.

'Woke up this morning'

Woke up this morning
In the middle of winter
Salt in my coffee
Sweat in my hair.
The letter said: She's dead,
We know you will miss her.
Woke up this morning
In winter in winter.

Started my answer
But failed to remember
The sound of her voice
Or the shape of her head.
Wrote I was sorry
Will be there on Thursday
Found myself busy
Sent flowers instead.

Several years later
I met her while dreaming.
Fingernails bitten
Her hands in her hair,
Lovely as ever:
I have to get started!
She shouted: *Get started!*
And parted the air.

Woke up this morning
In the middle of winter
Salt in my coffee

Sweat in my hair
All I could think of
Was sleeping beside her
And how she wore nothing
In winter in winter.

Eight from *Red Bird*

Lithe girl, brown girl,

the sun that makes apples
and stiffens the wheat
made your body with joy.

Your tongue like a red bird
dancing on ivory,
your lips with the smile of water.

Tantalize the sun, if you dare,
it will leave
shadows that match you, everywhere.

Lithe girl, brown girl,
nothing draws me towards you
and the heat within you
beats me home

like the sun at high noon.

Knowing these things,
perhaps through knowing these things,
I seek you out,

daft for the sound of your voice

or the brush of your arms against wheat,
or your step
among poppies grown under water.

Steep gloom among pine trees.
The waves surge breaking. Slow lights
that interweave. A single bell.
As the day's end falls into your eyes
the earth starts singing in your body
as the waves sing in a white shell.

And the rivers sing within you
and I flow outwards on them
as you direct them
whither you make them run;
I follow after like a hare
running reared upright to the hunter's drum.

You turn about me
like a belt of clouds. Your silence,
though it is stupid, mocks the hours I lay
troubled by nothing. Your arms
translucent stones wherein I lie
exhausted. And future kisses die.

Last, your mysterious voice folds close
echoes that shift throughout the night.
Much as the wind that moves
darkly, over the profitable fields,
folds down the wheat
for all its height.

That you may hear me, my words
   narrow occasionally,
like gull tracks in the sand.

  Or I let them become
tuneful beads mixed with the sound
   of a drunk hawk's bell
fit for your wrists.

  And soft as grapeskin, yes,
softer than grapeskin I make them,
   which is a kind of treachery
against the painful world.

  Yet, you who clamber
over old desolations of mine,
   gentle as ivy, eat the word's meaning.

Before you came to me
   words were all you now occupy,
and now they know more,
   these words,
than ever they knew of my sadness.

  Yet, sometimes
the force of dead anguish
   still drags them and, yes,
malevolent dreams still, at times,
   overwhelm them, and then
in my bruised voice you hear

other bruised voices, old agues crying
out of old mouths.

   Do not be angry with me
lest the wave of that anguish drowns me
   again. Even as I sit
threading a collar of beads for your neck
   softer than grapeskin
hung with a drunk hawk's bell.

Drunk as drunk on turpentine
from your open kisses,
your wet body wedged
between my wet body
and the strake of our boat
that is made out of flowers –
feasted, we guide it (our fingers
like tallows adorned with yellow metal)
over the sky's hot rim
the day's last breath in our sails.

Pinned by the sun between solstice
and equinox, drowsy and tangled together
we drifted for months and woke
with the bitter taste of land on our lips,
eyelids all sticky, and we longed for lime
and the sound of a rope
lowering a bucket down its well. Then,
we came by night to the Fortunate Isles,
and lay like fish

under the net of our kisses.

Sometimes it's like you're dead
when you say nothing

or you heard things I say
and couldn't be bothered to reply

and your eyes, sometimes,
move outside of you
watching the two of us, yes,

as if
after you turned towards the wall
somebody's kisses stopped your mouth.

My fingers have crept
down your body's white map
like patient spiders

and my tongue has worked
innumerable tales
to make you glad.

Yet you are never glad,
or longing, or kind, or dear.
Nor will you go away.

And if I kill your father
they will kill me. So,
let us try again.

Wings whirr by moon and midnight,
slatted moon is notched into the pine's bark,
pines used as masts are varnished by the level moon,
sails like enormous flakes of rust. A bird,

hovering, hovering, close to the bollards.

Now the wind keeps time in the lion's
iron ears while the sunshine flakes his hide
cast from similar metal, and the bronze ring
set loose between his teeth, feels no spittle.

Your mouth is loose and wet, and my mouth
covers it like a rag, dryly. Bells toll.
The sun struggles to rise – it is hard – and, rising,
sillies the moon. Birds drown. Breath smells.

No matter how hard you scream,
the lion will not wake, the masts not curve,
nor will the pine's bark fall across
your lime-white throat, delicately. And if

our body shouted out with both its voices,
there is not breath enough to fill
even the smallest sail, so
you may as well sleep here, one

of this love's poor twins who gasp
around their four-armed cradle where
birds are strangled by the woman's hair
and the man blames her.

Tonight, I write sadly. Write
for example: Little grasshopper
shelter from the midnight frost
in the scarecrow's sleeve, advising myself.

The night wind throbs in the sky.

Tonight, I write so wearily. Write
for example: I wanted her
and at times it was me she wanted. Write,
the rain we watched last fall

has it fallen this year too?
She wanted me, and at times it was her
I wanted. Yet, it is gone, that want.
What's more, I do not care.

It is more terrible than my despair
at losing her. The night, always vast,
grows enormous without her, and
my comforter's tongue talking about her

is a red fox barred by ivory. Well,
does it matter I loved too weak to keep her?
The night ignores such trivial disputes.
She is not here. That's all.

Far off someone is singing.
And if to bring her back I look
and I run to the end of the road
and I shout, shout her name,
my voice comes back: the same, but weaker.

The night is the same night; it whitens
the same tree; casts the same shadows.
It is a dark, as long, as deep, and as endurable
as any other night. It is true: I don't want her,

but perhaps I want her . . .
Love's not as brief that I forget her,
so. Nevertheless, I shall forget her, and
alas, as if by accident

a day will pass in which
I shall not think about her even once.
And this the last line I shall write her.

Gone Ladies

Where in the world is Helen gone
Whose loveliness demolished Troy?
Where is Salome? Where the wan
Licentious Queen of Avalon?
Who sees my lady Fontenoy?
And where is Joan, so soldier tall?
And She who bore God's only Boy?
Where is the snow we watched last Fall?

Is Thaïs still? Is Nell? And can
    Stem Héloïse aurene,
Whose so-by-love-enchanted man
Sooner would risk castration than
    Abandon her, be seen?
Who does Scheherazade enthral?
And who, within her arms and small,
    Shares Sappho's evergreen?

Through what eventless territory
Are ladies Day and Joplin swept?
What news of Marilyn who crept
Into an endless reverie?
You saw Lucrece? And Jane? And she,
Salvation's ancient blame-it-all,
Delicious Eve? Then answer me:
Where is the snow we watched last Fall?

Girl, never seek to know from me
    Who was the fairest of them all.
What wouldst thou say if I asked thee:
    Where is the snow we watched last Fall?

Nell's Circular Poem

she came to me in the middle of winter,
two-thirds my age, wearing a furry hat.
When she is happy her smile is like
that of the flower girl who tiptoes up
and down the lawn, and somewhat to the right
of Botticelli's Graces in his *Spring*.
And when she thinks, her upper lip gets thin;
and somewhere in between her nose and chin
a delicate obsession floats.
She blinks a lot. Is punctual. And I love her.

Now it is ten years later to the day.
I answer less. My pubic hair is grey.
And differently I love her more than when

Epitaph

I am old.
Nothing interests me now.
Moreover
I am not very intelligent
and my ideas
have travelled no further
than my feet.
You ask me:
What is the greatest happiness on earth?
Two things:
changing my mind
as I change a penny for a shilling;
and
listening to the sound
of a young girl
singing down the road
after she has asked me the way.

Singles

I was one
among 2000 million.
I read diverting books
when nine-tenths of the rest
had not been taught to read.
Enjoyed my work
when two-thirds of the rest
were unemployed.
Ate often, well, when half the rest
went hungry.
And knowing that my ways lacked right
I promised: Change comes soon.
Yet slept eight easy hours each night —
and one each afternoon.

I live a life of almost total idleness.
My friends grow silent.
My enemies rejoice.
But luckily my mind is fogged
by vanity and pride
so I see nothing.
'Alas, my son,' my mother says,
'your case is hopeless . . .'
Her cheekbones glisten in the neon dusk.
'Unhook your ear and blow your nose, old bag,' I say —
but only to myself.

'Tis just as well
In the Customs shed
They search my bag
But not my head.

On days when I intend to work
I clean my room as if I were
expecting an important guest.
That done, I sit and ask myself:
    What can have kept her?

Even on the night
when the great wave smothered Atlantis
I shouted: 'More coffee!'

I like to think:
    were I a black I would be a Black Panther
    my hands would be hard from the art of karate
    my mind would be hard as the practice of Stalin
    and my heart would be harder than both.

But were that my case
    I would probably be
    an elderly bell-hop with: 'Yes, Mr Big!'
    for any white pig.

Her body makes me grateful to nature
and mindful of my own.
Her word part, her dumb part,
both delight me.
Lightly I touch her half parted lips
with the tip of my tongue.

If the nightflights keep you awake
I will call London Airport and tell them
to land their dangerous junk elsewhere.

And if you fall asleep with the sleeve
of my jacket under your head
sooner than wake you, I'll cut it off.

But if you say:
'Fix me a plug on this mixer,'
I grumble and take my time.

Nell,
coming to tell me:
'No.'
Now she has gone
the gate still swings.

Politely saying goodbye
I feel my hand go up in flames.

Last night in London Airport
I saw a wooden bin
labelled UNWANTED LITERATURE
IS TO PLACED HEREIN.
So I wrote a poem
and popped it in.

Last night in Notting Hill
I saw Blake passing by
who saw Ezekiel
airborne in Peckham Rye.

Fragment

It is time I got out.
It is time that I left this city.
For years I have quarrelled with everyone.
I wrote malicious things because
inflicting pain was agreeable
and the pay quite good.
Often as not the things I wrote
were stolen from better writers than me,
though sometimes lesser men served just as well.
Be that as it may, it is time I got out,
but I hate the countryside,
and the peasants scare me.

May the 14th
and a letter comes from my mother, saying:
'I went down to the hospital
and all they said was, well,
reaching your age our aches will be the same.
So that is that. I cannot knit.'

53 years I have been in your city
and still I do not know you, or your ways.
I talk too much; and when I talk
gesticulate too much; and slender booms
endlessly tending cinderbeds along the city's cut
affect me deeply.

What am I doing here, anyway?
After 53 years I represent no one;

I give no comfort; I produce no change.
No clamour of a common weal or woe
summons the lesser clamour of my tongue
to give its resolution clarity.
As for the part of shouting evil down,
my need of it is fading as the light
around the house that hides my failing fades
a little earlier each day as winter comes.

October. Late birds shake their wings.
There is a certain brightness in the air.
For those who wish to turn new minds to heaven
and not deny their ancestors, it says
that common celebration must fulfil
the perfect wording given to me by those
who wave from their allotments as the train goes by.

    Words. Open words. Closed words.
Shouts from a passing window. Things
wives hear about soon after lighting up.

    I have no taste for everlasting truth;
and they have other fish to fry.

    25,609
miles on the clock of my car.
Tomorrow is a mystery.
The past moves quietly away.
No one is asking me to stay.
And yet I do not go.

    Besides, where should I go?
My skin is white. My one good eye is blue.

With these most grievous signs against my kith
the time on earth still left to me
would pass explaining things away
that cannot be explained away.
Of course, I might pretend to be a Jew.
No, no – the risk is still too great,
as the rain rises on the dawn wind
and the gulls stall over Lambeth, where,
flat as a plank split by the sun's meridian
the river spills bright sheaves of water
on dependent sheaves
until the lighted estuary streams up the sky.

    One evening, through the windows of a house
whose garden trespasses on Primrose Hill
I saw a man in general's uniform
seated before a table spread with maps.
He had the dreamy gaze of one who'd crossed
the cinder basins of a planet where
sublime attempts were made to ruin war,
and now the given bearings of that march
bisect his waist (and he has double checked them, carefully)
realises he has lost his cavalcade:
his men, his wife, his child, his horse, his dog,
and finally, his reason.

    Filled with tears
to see this brave old man so troubled in the dusk,
I knocked, pointed towards the latch, and said:
before my words were out he drew the blind.

Blue light through pleached green.
Only the faraway race of an adding machine
through the architect-crafted factory's half
opened office block window today
being Sunday.

Silence that man.
How dare he call my idleness to mind.
Is it not half enough that all the world
sits hang hand idle on a day like this?
How it deprives my pleasure of its sting
knowing that all are idle, all.

Perhaps the man is clever?
Dare I drift tiptoe in some poolside thing,
and, where the outfall slides
over the trouty footage of the weir,
call out: 'I say –
three times as much as you are getting now
to follow me.'

Time flies.
Bats dip their wingtips in the starlit pool.
My towel stays moist.

How I detest this planet!
Fifteen governments have failed
to crown my head.
Despite my hangdog charm, my silver wit,
my small, consoling pout,
I compose these exquisite sentences
in clothes that are almost threadbare.
I have done my best to explain.

I have said:
'I only wanted to get my name in the papers.'
When nobody put my name in the papers
I refused to complain, I was patient.
But now that I cannot afford the papers
and have to rely on my landlord for news
my hope is most immeasurably low. My tears
fall quietly as hair
falls from a comb into the goose-necked pan.
Who will look after you when I have gone,
my verses?
Who will there be to like you when I make
that instant hole?

   The car arrives. I tell the driver: 'Jane,
we may fly home tomorrow. Hold the plane.'

New Numbers

'Comrades, let's face it – poetry as bad as this has not been seen in England since the 17th Century. A little more time, a little more patience, might have removed the worst of its faults; but the poet was well over 60 . . .'

Nine completely naked girls
will dance all Sunday afternoon
on the tomb of the Unknown Conscientious Objector.
In keeping with tradition
their profitable mounds will be close-shaved.
There will, however, be no posing.
Gooseflesh will rise to sumptuous music,
a melody of favourites played
by the Palace of Westminster steel band.
At three, a blind war hero
will leap onto the plinth and scream
'GOD WILL FORGIVE US ALL!'
The naked girls will trample him to death.
High in the freezing summer air
sixteen smiling constables will spray
hallucinatory vapours on the crowd
from US army helicopters.
And when these moistures bead their flesh
troubled enthusiasts will eat each other
raw.
At five, the People's Candidate
hot from the loss of his deposit in the East
will seize the microphone. His theme:
Council Housing For Child Murderers – A Beginning.

Next day a racist scholar will demand
increased grants for the parents of the dead.
A spastic faints outside the National Gallery.
Night falls. The sky is full of weeping reds.

Sodium lozenges. A car pulls in.
Half-parted silver lips. The hose.
   'You going far?'
   'Not far. I have to drive a friend to town.'
   'Good girl.'
Cannon the bonnet over two slow lanes.

TWO FAINT AT FUNERAL OF SNAKE
ZEN MONK DISCOVERED IN DÜSSELDORF SEWER
SPORTS-HERO SWALLOWS OIL SLICK
FAMOUS IDIOT JOINS CABINET
BIG RISE FOR SECRET POLICE
FIJI VANISHES
CENSOR PRAISES IGNORANCE
ALL MOUNTAIN TOPS OCCUPIED
BEDROOM FROLICS AFTER PARSNIP WINE
SELF DECEPTION — THE FACTS
PRODUCER CONDEMNS PLAYWRIGHT TO DEATH
'without taking the cigar from his mouth'
BLAKE SEEN OVER LONDON AIRPORT
LAST HORSE DIES
FUNERAL POORLY ATTENDED

Now and again a plane flies overhead.

Friday. Wet dusk.
Three blind men outside an Indian restaurant.
They shout at each other.
They have been drinking.

While sticks wave in the doorway.
The place is almost empty.
They feel about the tables.
Two patrons draw their curries back.
They find a table near the door.
They telescope their sticks and wait.

Their order is: two eggs and chips, one curry.
Their chins are up.
Their mouths are open.
One drums the laminated calico.

Their plates arrive.

The taller of the egg men reads his chips.
He learns their number and their average size.
The other one eats furiously.
He who chose curry, stirs it, looking upwards.

Shots of the Himalayas line the walls.

The rapid eater finishes and listens to the first.
He hears a fork enter a chip.
He hears the chip approach and disappear
forever into his companion's mouth.
And as its mastication starts
his fork moves out
and spears the cluster of remaining chips
securing two.

He eats them both.

Yolk coagulates on his lapel.

The one with curry yawns.

None of them have removed their overcoats.

The masticator's fork returns,
touches the plate, lifts half an inch, dips in,
lifts, hesitates, swings to and fro,
then stabs the gobbler in his face.

All three get to their feet.

The curry man supplies the waiter with his purse.
Their sticks expand.

Outside
they start to shout obscene remarks.

Sunset on tinted glass. Lit pinnacles.
She steps through the warmth of exhaust pipes.

Bliss, bliss, to see
the light, light, fall
from heaven through your fair.
And bliss to see
your white breasts pour.
Light, light,
fall on . . .

A policeman is walking from London to Glasgow.
His handkerchief is wet with tears.
And as he walks he cries:

'I do not want to be cremated when I die.
I do not want to be buried in consecrated ground.
I want to be buried under the M1
where the traffic never stops.
Then those who drive this way can say:
"Round about here a policeman is buried.
He died of love".'

Three criminals were driving up to town
in a stolen car.
As they passed the policeman the first one shouted:
'GOODBYE FATHER!' and the second shouted:

'GOODBYE MOTHER!' and the third one shouted:
'GOODBYE, MY LOVE!'

Being in Italy she thinks of France.
'You have my number? I must go.
Remember me. And thankyou for the dance.'

'Dear Son:
I went down to the hospital
and all they said was: "Well, when we're your age
the pain will be the same." So that is that.
I cannot knit.'

They said: The pilot overshot.
They said: It was a holiday tragedy.
They said the names of those who died
were being held until the relatives had been informed.
They said we need a piece about the relatives.
They said the one to get is Mrs J.,
young, lost her husband and two kids,
they said that she lives here,
a glass front door set in a painted wooden frame
left slightly open, I go in.
The radio is on.

I have to shout 'Hello?' quite loud
before she says: 'Come up.'
She's on the bed half drunk
with new clothes strewn all over.
'You're from the women's paper, I suppose?
You want to know exactly how I feel about the crash?
Well this is how I feel.
I'm glad he died. I'm glad.
He hadn't touched me for three years.
As for his dirty kids, I hated them.
I'm glad they're dead and I've still got my looks
and £20,000.'

'I have a charming view.
Two rivers mixing with the sea. The Evening star.
There is a woman here whose only subject is herself.
    " . . . my spittle has a prophylactic tinct.
    My children's, too. Tomorrow I must call them. In Brazil.
    My nightmare is I shan't get through."
When will you come? Don't worry about money. I have some.'

Light follows light along the motorway.

'Dear Son:
I felt so low tonight I got my photos out.
You and my mother. Goodness me,
how nice you were in those far distant days.
But do not think that I am giving in.
I am up and down like a dog at a fair.'

He lived near here.
Before the war most people couldn't read.

My father came in with the paper
and this is what he said:
'Fetch Mary.'

She came in her blue.

There were four strange men in the room.
They looked in the tea my mother had made.
'Read it,' he said.

She was nine. We had the same stars.

And the article said
how a man had committed the act with his eldest
and when it was due he took her by tube
and the hospital was the one facing Parliament
and on his first visit he grabbed up the child
and ran past the nurses
and out of the place
and down to the river
and threw it right in.

My father gave Mary a penny for reading.
He smoked forty a day and got killed in the war.

'You remember that man they hanged for the drowning?'
my mother asked fifteen years later.

Mary had moved. I still have her card.

'We knew him.
His wife died of something. His eldest kept house.
She came here the evening they took him away.'

'If ever I go to a dance with Yvonne
– the loose one who bit herself off when the Yankees went home –
when I get back he is waiting.
He strips me and has me downstairs.
When he's finished he says:
What you give to them you'll give me too.

Except for this he's kind.
He calls me our mother
and gives me his wages unopened.

The funny thing is
no one had it but him.
Well, maybe a feel, but no more.'

'I have had my legs waxed and bought a new bikini.'

'. . . and yesterday
while hanging out my washing on the line
I was blown over by the wind . . .'

'You are accused – '
'Shut up you poof. You fucking poofter. Poof.'
'You are – '
'All right, I fuck you. Poofter fuck.'
'You understand – '
'That is the answer. Fuck you. Yes.'
'You – '
'I fuck you too. Fuck England. Fuck America.'

'Shall we assume he pleads not guilty?'

'Fuck you too.'

'Ask him again.'
'Poof. Ask yourself.'
'Ask him.'
'Bastard. bastard. bastard poof.'

Saying these things he dropped his shorts
shat in his hands
and frightening off his guards with it
stepped from his shorts

and strode with hands outstretched towards the magistrate
demanding to be treated with respect
demanding to be given the VC.

'Rain in September. In Tuscany. Would you believe it?
Here is my poem:
    Watch out, you toads! –
    Her Majesty the Folkswagen is coming . . .
Will your work help a body hoe their row?
Is your book a good book to have
when you are alone, in hospital, in a foreign country?'

Now and again a plane flies overhead

I have to tell you about Mr Valentine.
He was small. Very small. Very clean. Very
shy neat and smiling was he
Mr Valentine, who spent all of his days
regardless of where he might be
Topolobambo or Juba or Penge
looking for someone. His darling. His love.
Very small. Even smaller than he.
Tiny lips tiny teeth tiny breasts tiny feet
mini most mini but perfectly made.

He could not find her.

One day he climbed to the top of a bus,
in London it was, before it blew down.
The upstairs was empty. He chose the back seat.
Looking out of the window to find her
   My darling! My darling!
His love.

Up the stairwell came Ruby.
Big Ruby. Huge Ruby. Enormous strong Ruby
with hair on her arse.
She put down her shopping and grabbed Mr Valentine
up by his handstitched lapels and said:

   'M I N E'

There was no one about.

   'Ring the bell, Mr V. The next stop is ours.'
They got off. They walked down the road.
They got married.

Clouds overcame the marvellous sun.

They went to her house. A neat house. A small house.
A house that was meant for a man just like him.
Mr Valentine, but
Ruby was big and he was so small
he had to sleep on the crust of the mattress.

   'Make love to me, Valentine. Kiss me all over,'
she'd say. And he did.

'Make love to me, Valentine. Kiss me all over.'
What else could he do?
It was awful, until
one day as he kissed her and stroked her and licked her
he started this theme:

   'I am walking in fields,' said Valentine, 'fields,
here is a pathway, there is a tree
with a brook passing by,
and there is a hillside all moony, like Palmer'
(see Wordsworth & Wordsworth,
a team who can do that stuff better than me).

One day by mistake
(except no one makes that kind of mistake)
while walking and dreaming he found it. His ingle.
A place all overgrown with odorous plants
that curtain out the day with leaves and flowers,
where a fountain sprang with awakening sounds.
He loved it. He stayed there all day.

   'Where have you been?' said Ruby.
   'Oh . . . nowhere.'
   'Where's *nowhere*?'
   'Oh nowhere.'

And each day thereafter he went there alone.

Near to the ingle an Irishman lived.
They called him Red Mick.
Mick's prick was as long as a baby's arm
hanging o'er the side of a pram.
He scared Mr Valentine stiff.

'You should meet Ruby.'
'Whose Ruby?'
'My Ruby.'
'That cow with the whopping great tits?'
'You've got it.'
'I'd sure like to fuck her.'

So when he got home Mr Valentine said:
  'A gentleman of my acquaintance loves you.'

  Ruby said nothing.
  'He's mad for you Ruby.
  'I feel sure you would like him much better than me.'
  'What's his name?'
  'He's called Eire. Incarnadine Eire. He's Irish.'
  'THAT bastard?'
  'Oh, Ruby . . .'
  'He's only after one thing.'
  'Oh Ruby, dear Ruby . . .'

And just like a woman she stuck to her word.
But she wanted to know where Valentine went.

  'Just wait by my ingle, Red Mick.
  Sooner or later she'll follow, I promise.'
  'OK.'
And she did.

She saw him go under the odorous plants.
She tried to get in.

Mr V. in the foreground.
   'Come out here this instant!'
Mr V. stepping backwards.
   'Come out here I say!'
She thrusts her head forwards.
Another step backwards.

   'Come out here!
   Come out here!
   Come, oh, Mr Valentine, help me
   I'm stuck!'
And she was.

Up came Red Mick and lifted her skirt.
   'You rapist! You monster!
   You worse than the beasts!'
As he skinned off her knickers of dayglo green.
   'Stop it you bastard! I hate you! I hate you!'
Shrieked Ruby.
But nobody came.

So Red Mick impaled her and Valentine kissed her
and told her old stories and tickled her chin.
And the fountain made its awakening sounds
as water alone can sing in this world.

   'You bastard,' said Ruby, but softer,
   'You swine . . .'

And Valentine looked in her eyes and saw mist.

Late afternoon and they went to her house,
Red Mick and Big Ruby. They're living there yet.
They fight, but who cares?

Mr V. felt alone. A bit sad. But relieved.
He straightened his tie
and started to look for his darling again.

Gunfire disturbs the dawn.
·Helmeted men examine lengths of tangled hose.

'. . . you must forgive this being typed (by Christopher).
How I should love to see you all. But I can picture you
where from our table we could see all Malaga.
Now, Carmen dear, I must stop writing.
It pains my arm and takes about an hour to go away.
My prayers are yours.
Your English mother for a little while,
and for all time, your friend.'

'Boy, clear your plate! Believe you me,
you will not leave this table till you do.'

Roadblocks surround the city. Bowsers on runways.

Last night, as I lay waiting at the verge of sleep
I saw an angel lift her hand towards a drape
gather its fall aside
then beckon me forwards with her head.
There, in full sunlight, the Atlantic lay,
a liner in its midst.
And on the liner's afterdeck
(dressed in a linen suit and canvas-topped shoes)
T. S. Eliot
reading, smiling.

'I am fed up with you.
You say you love me but you do not come.
Yet you complain I have another man.
I do not have *another man*.
I sleep around because I hate to sleep alone.
Sleeping alone means that I do not sleep,
or pills.
So do not act the jealous boy.
Come now. At once. Today.
We will do this: travelling, we help
those who need help,
but ask for nothing in return.
Children whose files are inches thick,
impatient men who cannot change a wheel,
still travelling on and on until we die.'

A Greek who made millions in shipping
is walking alone by the sea.
It is autumn. Near sunset. The wind has died down.
Raising his eyes from his white
basketweave shoes
he sees a boat come gliding in on two bright foils
its blue patrol lamp flashing.
And in the wheelhouse of the boat
a man in uniform is singing
what the Greek will later describe
as a song of great beauty, not sad.
Listen to what the millionaire said:
'I will give you the earth if you sing it again.'
And the man said: 'I will,
if you sail with me.'

Morale being low a decision was made
for a cargo of whores to be sent to the troops
but it sank (in a fog) on the rocks
and the women (none of them young) were drowned
but were not brought ashore.
So for more than a week
their bodies were seen by the soldiers
sometimes in clusters sometimes alone
their peroxide hair spread out on the waves.

'I loathed your call.
Of course I was polite.
Now I am not.
Pick – if you must – fights with yourself
But do not turn your nastiness on me.
What is this *home* you say I must come *home* to?
I have no home.
You come to me.
You understand?
You come to me.
Because of you I left
my jacket and my camera in the post office.'

The city dreams around you.
Tall red waves with faces in their crests
collapse among the tower blocks.
The faces are the faces of your friends.
One lifts his hat to you and says: 'Remember us.'
Then they are gone.
The sky is crowded with colossal masks
much like those faces drawn in chalk
that drift from left to right across your dark
as you lie waiting on the verge of sleep.

A sergeant of the police
fell madly in love with his daughter
a girl of fourteen.

All through the summer he lay upstairs
beneath a light blue counterpane.

The heat was terrible.
But the sound of her feet on the lino was worse.

'What is the matter with him, dear?
Doesn't he care about you or the force?'
'I don't know, mother. I just don't know.'

That evening she made him a pudding,
just as he liked it, with custard, no skin.
'Would you like some of this, dear?'
'Yes. I'd like it.
Let Betty bring it up when she comes in.'

It was summer. Late August.
Betty was wearing her gym slip and knickers.
She carried the food on a brown tin tray.

As she came through the bedroom door he grabbed her,
and fucked her and fucked her,
screaming:

'Let punishment come from above
because there is none on earth!
Let if all on my stinking wife.
She is to blame for everything!'

'Is something wrong?'
'You go.'
'What is it?'
'Nothing. Go alone.'
'You will enjoy it when you get there.'
'No.'
'Of course you will.'
'No. No.'

' . . . blown over by the wind
while hanging out my washing on the line.
But now I am properly dressed, and by my fire.
God bless dear Lilian.'

'I need a drink

I mean, I have been drinking.

I mean that I am drunk.'

'Oh come . . .'

'I mean I am a drunkard.
Drunk. An alcoholic. Drunk.
Look in my bag. Vodka. No ice.
I have been drunk since I got up.'

Tomatoes on toast in the still of the night
reading Milton.
You have grown old. 'That old guy with the book.'
You heard it in a queue and felt afraid.

'. . . for god's sake leave me *alone*.
I am weak. I have lost my looks.
I cannot get on with myself.
Day after day I stare at the oven.'

Dogs howl beneath high windows
and the cries of people being tortured fill the air
and the cries of their torturers drown them out
but they cry even louder
and their torturers go mad with frustration
and the girl who read your hand
in that milk bar in Wrexham,
what happened to *her*?

Will my work help you hoe your row?
Are mine good books to have
when you are ill in bed in a foreign country?

inside the station it was dark.
Me without luggage, under seventeen,
watching a man well over seventy years
ascend the decorated stairs that lead
onto the taxi ramp, pause at the top,
then looking back at me across the vast
half-empty booking hall, give one brief wave
as if it was an ordinary day
and not the last of many, or the first,
perhaps the only time that he had asked
something of me, before he disappeared
between the pillars of the broad arcade
whose leafy capitals support the dark glass vault
that keeps all weathers from this terminus.
The youth says *No.* The old man goes. And then
like light I flew towards him as he bent
into the taxi-cab, and said:
'I love you more than anyone in all the world.'
And now he holds me in his arms
and now I know he is about to die
and as they drive away, I wake.

What hopes I had when I came to the city!
My typewriter! My £50!

The Girls

By the weir it says: DANGER.
Chromium fittings wink from the opposite bank.

   I can borrow his car. Are you on?

Sun like ripe tungsten edged with wax polish
and in the middle air
gliders discover mosque-coloured thermals
on a day when sunlight makes water taste dry.

   I have something to tell you. A secret.

NO COACHES

   She sees far too much of that girl.

And her grandmother said:

   You can never be sure when something will happen.

   You drive.
   Will he mind?
It is low as a toy.
   Will he know?

The fake hide is hot and slightly adhesive.
It sears her
   Hang on!
while she braces, then

Better?
You bet.
and they go.

Silk
blotting the small of her back
on the lip of the coachwork, her forearm,
palm half raised, fingers parted for cooling,
a chill, flowered sweat in each fork.

You had something to tell me? A secret?
For later.
They are really quite close, but nothing has happened.
We might get a boat.
Can you row?

The driver nods. Her shoes are off.
Ask how she drives, she answers: Fast and safe.

Those fucking morons in their caravans!

You like my hair this way?
Clean bands of wand mascara guard each lid.
You like it long?
Edges and scents divide her from the world.
Perhaps it needs a cut.

So brightly the sun between leaves
they seem black. Gates painted green
other cars other cars
and between them the white, misty wealth
of homes set on golf-grass, well back from the road

and where, to the right, behind elm trees, the sky
leaps upward from the river's diamond head
sunbeams prosper on hand-stitched surfaces
oval enlargements glide over linen,
they park.

Cash. Cap.
   I have your bag.
Doors thock. Thighs glare through cotton filters.
Eyes abound.
   You keep the key.
They wade through chrome.

'WHEN GOD SAYS *YES* – SAY *YES* TO GOD.'

Leaves mute the weir. Its waters sound
like cola seething in a paper cup,
mixed with a choir that sings through tiny grilles:
   '*It is not dying,*
   It is not dying.'

   I could do with a lolly.
   Get two.

Three boating oafs enjoy a dirty joke.
She says: Which way to find the boats? Then bobs
(someone would like to punish her in silk)
along the catwalk to the brink.

Some 50 yards north west,
a queue for Mr Softee.

Purse in her hand

   [119]

pin in her mouth
head to one side
squeaky clean hair leaning out
does the comb leave red tracks
does her scalp like the feel of its teeth?
Rubber snaps.

Behind her in the queue a man in serge
his inside pocket filled with naked prints.
And as she peels the ice
and as the feasting surface of her tongue
flickers along its smoky pole
– O, he could take such shots of it,
shots called: I love your tongue,
I love its tip, O office butterfly!

She fears his eyes. She needs her friend. She goes
quickly towards the river's brink
and ivies lick her cheeks like tiny fish.
Weeks later in a crowded auditorium
masked by the cheering voices his will shriek:
'SUCK THIS – YOU FUCKSOME BITCH! SUCK THIS!'
and as the anthem fans their politics:
'BITCH! BITCH! BITCH! BITCH!'
and then she hears his vicar's sandal creak
and as she runs toward her friend
and as her friend's well-bitten fingertips
dandle her frightened scents from bank to peak
triangles blind his lens
and laughter stripes his mind.
And as her friend unties
and as she hops the peak
and as they glide away, away, she stoops.
    'Goodbye to him.'

Water. Spring water. Is lucid. Bends sunlight.
Strongly it mirrors. Substances change in its hand.

Three miles downstream
a boy has risen from his bed
taken his sub-machine-gun from its box
pulled on his shirt and gone
to the stable with sleep in his eyes.

The water flows east; she is rowing; she thrusts;
white straps dangle latches; opulent flesh wells over elastic;
and the one they call pretty just sprawls
saying nothing, but nothing, her eyes saying nothing
and behind them the sound of the weir fades to nothing
and above them the noise of a plane no one sees.

Cut to the boy. He cinches. He mounts.
Behind him the house is asleep under shutters.
He is nine. About nine. He knows the horse well.
How it stops. How it stands to the gate. And how,
as he touches the latch with his toe,
it sniffs, passes through, and turns west on the towpath.

    Is somebody calling?

Blade water light beneath blade metal edge.
Water evolving dark whorls in their wake.
Oars easily buried, length bent by the light
pulled through the water's continual door

by her body's soft lever up, into sunlight
it rises, she rises, eyes pour over fists into eyes
as the varnished prow splits miraculous dust
on the other girl's insteps, her thighs,
as she curves in the heat amid pillows.

The sun has moved west. It aims at the boy.
See the gun on his knees. See the horse,
how it steps through the nettles.

   Is somebody calling?

And the sky is an empty blue jar.
And the high, wooden strakes of their fortress touch heaven.
And aside from the light
occasional drip of an oar, all is silent.

   I'm so hot.
   So am I.

and glides from her blouse
though the world sees no more than an elbow

   You had something to tell me? A secret?

on the curve of her pupil the other girl's lips

   Last night I was tired. Dead tired.

her fingers unlocking a column of teeth

I got up.
I was naked and sweaty.

I went to the kitchen.

there are leaves on the water

Go on.

And when I came up –
From the kitchen? –
The kitchen

the leaves on the water

his door was half open.

her father's

He sleeps on his own.
It's years since he touched her.

her mother

Go on.

the leaves on the water

He was sleeping on top of the clothes.
I went in. With the milk in my hand.
Something pushed me.

leaves high on the water

    I looked at his . . . I –
    I wanted to . . .
    Tell me. I love you. Please tell me.
    I wanted to –

all of a sudden

    And did you? And did you?

all of a sudden they twirl through the reeds
and vanish away.

The gun is elegant.

Born to the meditations of a man
who lived between the wars in Germany,
its moving surfaces required exactitude
measured to tens of thousandths of an inch
before the boy on indoor days could watch
the apparition of his vacant face
hover beneath its oily sheen.

    Is somebody calling

    And did you? And did you?

Blood tests do not reveal the past.
Much of his parents' time is spent abroad.

But in the house with the shutters always closed
a woman called Lacksheesh
feeds him, and cuts his fingernails, and sings.

Immovable heat. The water is foil. Wing becomes leaf.
Insects are gemstones.

   I love you.
   I love you.

   Is somebody calling?

No sound from the earth and the light is like oil.
   I love you.
   I love you.

His ears mark the source, he rides forward.

   I love you.
   I love you.

And the reeds smell of autumn already,
and the water between them is still,
and the reeds stretching down through the water,
its stillness, their stillness, repeating
shots of his father's tall-faced horse
with the rushes piercing its neck.

Advancing kisses thread the image of her body
to their tip. Suspended on that tip, her scents,
her coloured textures, day and age, are weightless names
flicked backwards into nothingness away.
And as the sunlight mutters in her throat

her spine's arched lance
presents its centre to the vivid bud.

The boy sees fish: innumerable fish
crushed by the surface as their moat is drained.
Fishes that boil and suffocate, that dive through fish.
Fish wallowing on fish, with other fishes kicking in their jaws.
The slap of desperate fish that half rise up,
and up, as if to pitch their shiny effluent
over the riverbank and him.
The gun keeps time.
Echoes that question the daylight's priority
flee under miles of greenish cloud
toward the known world's end.
And as the bullets squeeze into the light,
their leader sends the first
of many cone-shaped waves across the air.
And through that funnel apex after apex drifts
aimlessly on towards the girls.

The sky begins to fall. Thick drops, and slow,
round, heavy, sensual drops; fat drops
that waver in the quietude, that pause
a moment, pause a moment, pause, and then
divide into that kind of hammering rain
old men forget until the end of their reunion.
Tree crests explode. The river's surface smokes,
so wedded to the air you cannot see
the child urge his horse across the stippled brink.

Widespread upon the river's cloudy fall,
heavy as white, wet, winestained bread they lie.
And though the smudge they make is lost in rain,

and clouds, divided by long vents of slating gray
reflect that time when late birds swoop in threes
towards the fading image of the hills,
the boy can see their fingers, beckoning.
And, as the horse turns back, can hear his name
lovingly called by those who lead the way.

Late on the kind of summer afternoon
when intermittent rain has kept us in,
the sky is sometimes emptied from above,
and, hoping for an hour in the sun,
until we reach the open, fail to see
the day has entered into evening while we sat.
Reaching the bank we find the river full;
broader than we remembered it; quite still.
The land is there to frame the estuary.
The estuary to underwrite the sky.
Everything makes us certain night will fall
without a sign of life on either hand.
And we are on the point of leaving, when,
just for an instant something emerald flares
among the crosslights rising off the sea
and exits through the seamless curvature
of water mixed with sky and quiet stars.

Urbanal

The slippery whinnock, clear across the way,
Has had my tree cut down.
He rang a man who rang a man who knew
A big-boned, broad-backed chap; the type of clay
That stood in red in line at Waterloo.
It took eight hours to knock King Boney down,
And more than 30 years to rear my tree;
But only fifteeen dental seconds flat
For that, fat, jelly-baby-faced,
Pornocrat to have it stapped.
    Now I can see his house.
A snot-brown, lie-priced, isometric blob
Smack in the middle of my laureate eye.
A yawning house, a stealthily maintained,
And as (God stop his heart) he skives abroad
A semi-empty house. His swap. Who had my tree's
Shoulders that made the evening summer breeze
Hiss like a milky night-tide up the sand
Cut down to save his garage.
    Its roots were getting at his garage.
His garage was endangered. Furthermore,
Come autumn, when the bronzed wing in, his car
Might get its chrome trim splashed with flock.
    What can I do?
Twice 20,000 square in legal blue
Behind the leaves that bear his signature
And all my leaves away.

True, there are quits.
Through the enormous windows of his house
Soon after dusk when all was still and glad,
Five weeks ago I tingled as I watched
A no less sturdy, somewhat different lad,
Slither the cutlery into his bag
And fade. And Sunday last
(Meantime his nanny milked my breakfast tea)
His 'Me! Me!' squeakers did their peevish best
To baste each other's shop-washed goldilux
With Hong-toy-Kong posh hand-assembled trucks.
    Such treats, however, will not quash his crime:
Indubitably I would have
Him and his pimply mouthpiece taken out
Put up against that garage wall, and shot,
If all those lads in red and blue were mine.

    And yet I did not know my tree too well.
I did not know its name; its proper age;
Whether its leaflike slips of polished silk
Were toothed or bayed, or if its full, fresh snood,
Brotherly hugged, flushed leek down green imperial;
Or did that gust strike dark down adder green? –
How much it gained each year; how high it stood;
Or standing might have fetched that fleshy hood,
Except he had it lamed, laid, lopped, and logged:
'Just for the wood'.

    Is there no law?
Can nobody make Somebody obey?
I love the law. I dream about the law.
Few inky maids can make me jaunt so. See:
    An army overspreads a treeless plain.

A king is up for swaps. Between the lines
Of yet to be committed soldiery,
Leading his horse, alone, a youngish man
(One of the Lord Protector's *Fervent Best*)
Confronts the Kirkish generals. Flintlocks hiss.
They bunch. They talk. They separate. They say:
'Where is your warrant for His Majesty?'
And hear him, as he draws his sword, say: 'This.'
And shamefaced watch him lead brave Charles away.

Rate me with those who pray
Beside the two-years-later headless king,
Or cine-see the Emperor rowed away,
Some worldoramic, pandimensional fling
Stayed by the rape that lies in melody,
And have your own sweet way. But say:
    Go visit City Hall, anonymously
And well prepared. Go shaved; go calm; go hat
In humble hand, and,
Hot for the dream that scragged regality
Reactivate a hidden bureaucrat
And, with his führerstat,
Enforce the preservation of your tree –
Or will, or may, or might, or soon, or must
Is all you get from me.

    Or say I did. And say,
Exploding with authority, I led
A cloud of geriatric minutemen,
Lewd, loonie nudists, snagged by plastic leaves,
Little old ladies looped to tree-trained dogs,
Dogs local, ex-police dogs, Dogs Resist,
A teacher of the Vegetative Tongue

Linked to a glamorous preservationist,
Two dozen twangling squatters, Puss & Purr,
Bucket disguised, and Dogberry serene,
Blake of *The Globe* (with its photographer)
Plus anyone who likes the colour green
Up to his mammoth sty? Why . . . fine prepaid,
With well greased sliders wide, that schnorkel he
Can tip his fag, look down, and obelise
All my sad riff-raff with impunity.

A curse upon the law. Where did I kiss
My right to cut that scumbag down goodbye?
If I am weak (and certainly
My eye at sunset can no longer fix
A late bee backing from a mile-off rose)
Sly murder haunts my mind. And yet to lie
For all the world's great-headed blossomers
One of a long-forgotten laughing stock
Locked in a laughing house for aye?
Not bloody me.

Twilight. The blind man's holiday.
Blurred moonshine in the dewy slate.
I am reduced to prayer. I pray:

Let the stump get him. Let him,
You hideous, mauve-lidded, high-rise sylphs,
Whilst he is gruntly drunkling for his key
Be lashed by instant withies to the sour
£X million an acre crud,
Stripped of his fancy tat, and left to rot.

Then, when the moon is cooked, and up the way
My neighbour and my neighbour's son perform
'Jerusalem' (for the umpteenth time) on flute
And English horn,
All through the winking night,
Until dear Lucifer is born
Again between the courthouse and the block,
And something less than dawn
But more than darkness strides from Ragstone Brock
Down and across my city's viewless lea,
Crank on his stump I rock,
Groaning upon my loss, and on the loss
To local poetry.

'O come all ye faithful'

O come all ye faithful
Here is our cause:
All dreams are one dream,
All wars civil wars.

Lovers have never found
Agony strange;
We who hate change survive
Only through change.

Those who are sure of love
Do not complain.
For sure of love is sure
Love comes again.

From Book XXI of Homer's *Iliad*

PRELUDE
As they returned towards the river Scamander, Achilles split the Trojan army; one half, chased back along the same lines the Greeks had taken yesterday when Hector split their front, ran over the fields towards Troy: the other half were sealed into a loop made by the Scamander.

Jammed close, these miserable troops slithered down the bank into deep water, screaming as they twisted away from each other, their weapons tangled up, hands snatching at chin-straps.

Into this confusion Achilles waded, hacking amongst the mass till his arms went numb and the Scamander ran like the gutter set in the floor of a slaughterhouse.

Up to this time the river had not taken sides: now, soiled by a Greek, Scamander began contriving ways to help the Trojans.

Such thoughts might well have come to nothing. But, while the river planned, Achilles speared Asteropaeus – the grandson of the river Axius – scooping in the man's belly till his vitals floated out like mauve welts along Scamander's bank. And not content with this, Achilles stripped his victim, stood on his chest and said:

'From a duck's egg, a duck. Doubtless his relative Scamander
Will cleanse this dead, wet, wreck of an obstinate man.
A River king came in his mother's mother's slit so, proud of it,
He went for me, the one plain King's grandchild, and got killed.
But the axioms commemorating divine peerage, state:
Children from Heaven's one plain King – like me, dead man –
Match above any River's boy exactly as
Above the world's rivers combined at their spring estuaries,
Stands Heaven, stands in Heaven, God.
Consider the Scamander, here. A fine example for any River.

A big River. Surely Scamander would have, if he could have,
Taken your part? Pah! . . . I hunt a hare with a drum.
Such opposites mock competition, yes, the Freshwater King,
Achelous himself, plus five wide oceans, plus, O –
Plus the whole damp lot, are good as dead
Faced with God's warning thunder.'
                                        Then Achilles,
Leaving the tall enemy with eels at his white fat
And his tender kidneys infested with nibblers,
Pulled his spear out of the mud and waded off,
After the deadman's troop that beat upstream
For their dear lives.
                        Glimpsing Achilles' scarlet plume
Amongst the clubbed bulrushes, they ran, and as they ran
The Greek got seven of them, swerved, eyeing his eighth, and
Ducked at him as Scamander bunched his sinews up,
And up, and further up, and further further still, until
A glistening stack of water, solid, white with sunlight,
Swayed like a giant bone over the circling humans,
Shuddered, and changed for speaking's sake into humanity.
And the stack of water was his chest; and the foaming
Head of it, his bearded face; and the roar of it –
Like weir-water – Scamander's voice:

'Indeed, Greek, with Heaven helping out, you work
Miraculous atrocities. Still, if God's Son
Has settled every Trojan head on you,
Why make my precincts the scupper for your dead inheritance?
Do them in the fields, Greek, or – or do them anywhere but here.
Thickened with carcasses my waters stiffen in a putrid syrup,
Downstream, the mouth cakes against standing blood-clots yet,
And yet, you massacre. Come, Greek, quit this loathsome rapture!'

Head back, Achilles cried:
'Good, River, good—and you shall have your way . . . presently.
When every living Trojan squats inside his city's wall.
When I have done with Hector, Hector with me, to death.'
                    And he bayed and leapt –
Bronze flame shattering like a divine beast –
Pity the Trojans!

                    So Scamander
Tried involving the Lord Apollo, thus:
                    'Lord, why the negligence?
Is this the way to keep your Father's word?
Time and again he said: Watch the Trojan flank
Till sundown comes, winds drop, shadows mix and lengthen,
War closes down for night, and nobody is out
Bar dogs and sentries.'

                    Hearing this
The Greek jumped clear into the water and Scamander
Went for him in hatred: curved back his undertow, and
Hunched like a snarling yellow bull drove the dead up
And out, tossed by the water's snout on to the fields;
Yet those who lived he hid behind a gentle wave.
Around the Greek Scamander deepened. Wave clambered
Over wave to get at him, beating aside his studded shield so,
Both footholds gone, half toppled over by the bloodstained crud,
Achilles snatched for balance at an elm – ah! – its roots gave –
Wrenched out – splitting the bank, and tree and all
Crashed square across the river; leaves, splintered branches
And dead birds, blocking the fall. Then Achilles wanted out.
And scrambled through the root's lopsided crown, out of the ditch,
Off home.

But the river Scamander had not done with him.
Forcing its bank, an avid lip of water slid
After him, to smother his Greek breath for Trojan victory.
Aoi! – but that Greek could run! – and put and kept
A spearthrow's lead between him and the quick,
Suck, quick, curve of the oncoming water,
Arms outstretched as if to haul himself along the air,
His shield – like the early moon – thudding against
His nape-neck and his arse, fast, fast
As the black winged hawk's full stoop he went –
And what is faster? – yet, Scamander was nigh on him,
Its hood of seething water poised over his shoulderblades.
Achilles was a quick man, yes, but the gods are quicker than men.
And easily Scamander's wet webbed claw stroked his ankles.

You must imagine how a gardener prepares
To let his stored rainwater out, along
The fitted trench to nourish his best plants.
Carefully, with a spade, he lifts the stone
Gagging the throat of his trench, inch by inch,
And, as the water flows, pebbles, dead grubs,
Old bits of root and dusts are gathered and
Swept along by the speed of it, until
Singing among the plants, the bright water
Overtakes its gardener and his control
Is lost. Likewise Scamander took Achilles.

Each time he stood, looking to see which Part, or whether
Every Part of Heaven's Commonwealth was after him,
The big wave knocked him flat. Up, trying to outleap
The arch of it, Scamander lashed aslant and wrapped his knees
In a wet skirt, scouring the furrows so his toes got no grip.
And Achilles bit his tongue and shrieked: 'Father . . .'

Into the empty sky '. . . will Heaven help me? No?
Not one of you? Later, who cares? But now? Not now. Not this . . .'
Why did my lying mother promise death
Should enter me imaged as Lord Apollo's metal arrowheads?
Or Hector, my best enemy, call Hector for a big hit
Over Helen's creditors, and I'll go brave.
Or else my death is waste.
Trapped like a pig-boy beneath dirty water.

                              In Heaven, two heard him:
First, the woman Prince, Athena; and with her came
Fishwaisted Poseidon, Lord of the Home Sea.
And dressed as common soldiers they came strolling by,
And held his hand, and comforted him, with:
'Stick, my friend, stick. Swallow the scare for now.
We're with you and, what's more, God knows it, so
Stick. This visitation means one thing – no River
Will put you down. Scamander? . . . He'll subside. And soon.
Now child, do this: Keep after him no matter what.
Keep coming, till – I use your own fine words –
Every living Trojan squats inside his city's wall
And Hector's dead. You'll win. We promise it.'

  So the Greek, strong for himself, pushed by, thigh deep,
Towards the higher fields, through water
Bobbing with armoured corpses. Sunlight glittered
Off the intricate visions etched into breastplates
By Trojan silversmiths, and Trojan flesh
Bloomed over the rims of them, leather toggles sunk
To the bone. Picking his knees up, Achilles, now
Punting aside a deadman, now swimming a stroke or two,
Remembered God's best word and struck
Like a mad thing at the river. He beat it

With the palm of his free hand, sliced at it,
At the whorled ligaments of water, yes, sliced at them, Ah! –
There, there – there, and – *there* – such hatred,
Scamander had not thought, the woman Prince,
Scamander had not thought, and now, slice, slice,
Scamander could not hold the Greek! Yet,
Would not quit, bent, like a sharp-crested hyoid bone,
And sucking Achilles to his midst, called out:
'Simois, let's join to finish off this Greek – What's that?
Two against one, you say? Yes. Or Troy is ash,
For our soldiers cannot hold him. Quick, and help, come
Spanned out as a gigantic wave, foot up to peak
A single glinting concave welt, smooth, but fanged
Back in the tumultuous throat of it, with big
Flinty stones, clubbed pumice, trees, and all
Topped by an epaulette of mucid scurf to throttle,
Mash each bone, and shred the flesh and drown away
The impudent who plays at God.
Listen, Simois . . . Nothing can help him now.
Strength, looks – nothing. Why, that heavy armour, how
It will settle quietly, quietly, in ooze,
And his fine white body, aye, slimy and coiled up
I'll suck it down a long stone flue,
And his fellow Greeks will get not one bone back,
And without a barrow to be dug can save their breath for games.'

                                        And the water's diamond head
Shut over Achilles, locked round his waist
Film after film of sopping froth, then
Heaved him sideways up while multitudinous crests
Bubbled around his face, blocking his nostrils with the blood
He shed an hour before.

                        Then Hera, Heaven's queen,
Looked over the cloudy battlements of Paradise
And saw it all and saw the Greek was done and cursed Scamander,
Turned to Hephaestus her son, balanced on a silver crutch
And playing with a bag of flames, who, when his mother
Beckoned with her head, came close and listened:
'Little Cripple, would you fight Scamander for me?
Yes?' – rumpling his hair – 'You must be quick or' –
Giving him a kiss – 'Achilles will be dead. So,
Do it with fire, son; an enormous fire, while' –
Twisting his ear a bit – 'I fetch the white south wind to thrust
Your hot nitre among the Trojan dead, and you must
Weld Scamander wet to bank – now! But . . .
Wait. Little One, don't be talked out of it, eh?
More gods are threatened than struck, Scamander's promises
Are bought. Now, off with you, and, one last thing –
Sear him, Hephaestus, till you hear me shout!'

                        And the Fire God
From a carroty fuse no bigger than his thumb,
Raised a burning fan as wide as Troy
And brushed the plain with it until
Scamander's glinting width was parched
And smoke stopped sunlight.

                        Then the garnet-coloured bricks
Coped with whitestone parapets that were Troy's wall,
Loomed in smoky light, like a dark wicket bounding
The fire's destruction.
Troy's plain was charred and all in cinders
The dead Trojans and their gear. Yet Heaven's Queen
Did not call her son, and the Cripple
Turned on the beaten river.

Flame ate the elms,
Sad-willow, clover, tamarisk and galingale – the lot.
Rushes and the green, green lotus beds crinkled – wet dust,
The eels and the pike began to broil.
Last of all, Scamander's back writhed like a burning poultice,
Then, reared up, into a face on fire:
'How can I fight you, Cripple? Flames in my throat,
My waters griddled by hot lacquer! Quit – and I'll quit.
As for Troy and Trojans – let 'em burn. Are not we gods
Above the quarrels of mere humans?'

    You must imagine how the water
    For boiling down the fat of a juicy pig
    After the women pour it into a cauldron,
    Seethes and lifts as the kindling takes
    And the iron sits in a flamy nest.
    Likewise Hephaestus fixed Scamander.

    So the River God called to Heaven:
    'Queen, why does your boy pick on me?
    What of the other Gods who side with Troy?
    I promise to leave off if *he* leaves off. What's more
    I swear to turn away when Troy is burnt by Greeks.'

                So she called the Cripple off.
And between his echoing banks
    Scamander
Rushed gently over his accustomed way.

Notes

I would like to thank James Brady, James Campbell and Nicholas Jacobs for their help in compilling these notes.

Air 'Tom Beddoes', Thomas Lovell Beddoes (1803–1849) English dramatic poet.

Professor Tucholsky's Facts Kurt Tucholsky (1890–1935), German poet and satirist. Based on his essay 'Der Mensch', *Die Weltbühne*, June 1931, Vienna.

A Chorus from Antigone A version of the second Chorus from Sophocles' play.

Good Taste See *101 Zen Stories, Transcribed by Nyogen Senzaki and Paul Reps* (London, 1939) reprinted in *Zen Flesh, Zen Bones* (Rutland, Vermont, 1957).

The Song of Autobiography 'Ringarangaroo', a mildly obscene schoolboy song; *Envoi*, a version of the opening lines of Apollinaire's poem 'Vendemaire', *Alcools*, 1913.

A Singing Prayer The last four lines adapted from an inscription in Christchurch Priory (Hampshire) graveyard.

To My Fellow Artists Partly based on Bertolt Brecht's poem 'Rat an die bildenden Künstler, das Schicksal ihrer Kuntswerke in den kommenden Kriegen betreffend', *De Gedichte von Bertolt Brecht in einem Band*, Frankfurt-am-Main, 1981.

The Story of the Road 'Daniel', Danilo Dolci, the Italian social reformer who led the 'strike-in-reverse' that took place on 2 February 1956 and is described in the poem. See James McNeish, *Fire Under the Ashes*, 1965.

Caption for a Photograph of Four Organized Criminals A version of François Villon's poem 'L'Epitaphe, en Forme de Ballade', *Le Grant Testament*, 1461.

The Lily-White Boys   A musical produced in London in 1960, based on a play by Harry Cookson, the music by Tony Kinsey and Bill le Sage.

Rat, O Rat . . .   Based on a prose translation by G. L. Joerissen of Franz Touissant's French translation of Kong Tsie Tsan's (1207–56) poem 'A Petition'. See Joerissen's anthology *The Lost Flute*, 1923.

The Isles of Jessamy   'little shirt' = cutty sark. Of the *Cutty Sark*, the *Oxford Companion to Ships and the Sea* (ed. P. Kemp) says: 'The only survivor of the British tea clippers, now [1996] to be visited as a museum ship at Greenwich, London.'

Things   'Aston-Martin', an elegant, expensive, British sports-car.

Eight from Red Bird   Taken from a version of *Twenty Poems of Love and One of Despair* by Pablo Nerudu (1904–73) made by Patrick Bowles and me in 1954; revised by me in 1969.

Gone Ladies   A version of François Villon's 'Ballade des Dames du Temps Jadis', *Le Grant Testament*, 1461. 'Aurene' = shining gold; scans as in 'serene'.

'I was one'   The footnote to this poem reads:
  Admittedly admittances
  Like these do not increase
  Our chance of knowing if the I
  In question found release
  Through organized indifference
  Or gluttonous caprice.
  But they do something to explain
  His endless cries of 'Peace!'

'I like to think'   The Black Panther Party for Self-Defence, California, founded by Huey Newton and Bobby Seale in 1966, and named after the Black Panther Party of Lowndes County, Alabama. See Gilbert Moore, *A Special Rage*, New York, 1971.

New Numbers   'You are accused', etc., taken from a report of a trial before His Honour Judge Grubb at an Adelaide (Australia) court, May Session 1986. 'all overgrown . . .' to '. . . awakening sounds', see Shelley, *Prometheus Unbound*, III iii 11–14. 'Morale being low': this incident, in which a shipload of French prostitutes drowned when the vessel they were sailing in went down off the coast of Jersey, was called to my attention when published as an epigraph to a poem by Ann Harrigan in *Casablanca* 6, September/October 1993.

The Girls   'It is not dying', line 2 of John Lennon and Paul McCartney's lyric to their song 'Tomorrow never knows', *The Beatles Complete Works*, Amsterdam, n.d. (1969?).

Urbanal   'Whinnock' = the smallest pig in a litter. 'twice 20,000', the number of British police in 1975 – now nearer 70,000 and rising. 'An army . . .' to '. . . Charles away' described the arrest of King Charles I by Cornet Joyce at Holmby House (demolished), Northamptonshire, 4 June 1647. 'the Emperor', Napoleon I. 'Puss & Purr', two north-west London prostitutes advertised themselves under this title in 1969. 'obelise' = mark with a spit. 'Bucket', see Dickens, *Bleak House*. 'Dogberry', see Shakespeare, *Much Ado About Nothing*.

'O come all ye faithful'   the first line of the translation, by Fredrick Oakley, of 'Adeste, fideles', an anonymous Latin – now a famous English – hymn.